HOW TO LIVE
THE LIFE OF A MULTIMILLIONAIRE...
WITHOUT BEING ONE

CHRIS GRAY

Published in Australia by:

Go For Your Life Pty Ltd

Level 11, 66 Clarence St, Sydney NSW 2000

PO Box N64, Grosvenor Place NSW 1220

Phone: 02 9994 8944

www.yourempire.com.au

info@yourempire.com.au

ISBN: 978-0-6450869-0-4

Written by: Chris Gray

HOW TO LIVE
THE LIFE OF A
MULTIMILLIONAIRE...
WITHOUT BEING ONE

Fancy living in a house three times more expensive than you can afford to buy?

Want to know how owning a Lamborghini can be cheaper than buying a BMW or Mercedes?

Prefer to taste champagne on a luxury cruiser rather than sparkling wine in a tinny?

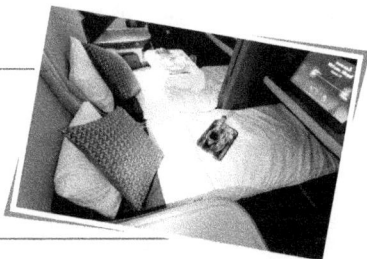

Would you rather fly business or first class for the same price as an economy ticket?

From other readers of "How to Live the Life of a Multimillionaire... Without Being One"

> As an adviser who manages money for high net wealth people, I ostensibly only have two questions I ask everyone:
>
> At what age would you like for work to be optional?

What level of passive income makes work optional for you?

The ultimate goal for all of us to is to get to that point where we can spend more time doing the things we love and hopefully afford to live the life we always wanted.

Within this book, Chris Gray covers his story about how he made work optional for himself, but moreover the keys to enjoying all the things you never thought you could, in a strategic, rational and economic way. Ever the contrarian, Chris dispels the myth that you must work forever and save your pennies for a future day, he covers the power of gearing, and shares how you can get on with life now, using the income you have.

Chris makes it clear that you don't need to be someone with $10mil of investments to enjoy life – simply use what you have in a more effective and considered way.

As investment managers, we believe in diversity, in holding different assets styles and types, but Chris via this book and his well renowned book *The Effortless Empire* shares how you can kickstart the journey of wealth creation using property and the power of gearing.

Charlie Viola
Partner
Pitcher Partners

From other readers of "How to Live the Life of a Multimillionaire... Without Being One"

You can have your cake...car, boat, house and chopper too. Chris Gray demonstrates how the everyday Australian can plan for their future while breaking down some of the old-fashioned bricks and mortar approaches to investment, rather than being tied to debt. Chris lives and breathes his strategies and is happily engaged in a very fulfilling life doing so.

Jacqui Clarke
Non-Executive Director
Maxima Private

What are people saying about Chris Gray?

If there's a way to boost income and profitability to allow more time for sitting around the pool and enjoying life, Chris will hunt it down! It's the only time you see him get off the deck chair. He's the master of work smart strategy.

Petrina Buckley
Co-founder -
Magneto Communications & Credosity

I have been following Chris' advice for over 15 years. I have used his books, seminars and social media advice to invest on Sydney's Northern Beaches and Inner West. What resulted was a multi million dollar property portfolio which allowed us to buy luxury yachts, cars and holidays for our family. Forever appreciative!

Todd Page
Sydney

CONTENTS

FOREWORD

I've never been one for clutter, and have always prioritised experiences over material things. I firmly believe experiences are what shape and develop us. We are a culmination of the stories we collect, the places we've been, and the things we've seen.

Fortunate to have lived a life full of experiences, I've travelled the world and absorbed as much as I could along the way. The diverse geographies, different cultures, languages, extremes in climate – every place and experience is unique. It is shared experiences that mean the most. "Do you remember the time etc" - what might be challenging in the moment becomes a great story retold over and over.

It led me to create RedBalloon over 20 years ago, as I wanted to shift the way people experienced life.

Now as Australia begins to emerge from the pandemic, there has been a significant shift in priorities. People have taken the time to reflect on what is important to them, and perhaps changed their view of work, life and play. Work used to be a place we went, now work is what we do. And experiences have never been in such demand. And RedBalloon of course makes it easy for people to know what they can do - and what is really great.

So if Chris Gray's book does nothing else, let it inspire you to live a life rich in experience. Dream, plan and explore, and get ticking some of those things off your own bucket list (you will be doing good by not just yourself, but businesses and the economy too).

What is something you have always wanted to do? Because today is the day to start planning it.

Naomi Simson,
Founder of RedBalloon

CHAPTER 1
WHY IT IS WORTH READING THIS BOOK?

Money isn't the answer to everything, but when you have ample cash at your disposal, it certainly is easier to have more freedom and choice in your life.

Over the last 30 years I've learnt that many people chase a dream of accumulating material items such as houses, cars, boats, watches, handbags, shoes - or whatever the indulgence might be - and once they've 'ticked them off their list', they often don't actually value or want them anymore.

Many wealthy people want to own their assets (and expensive toys) as a sign of achievement that also carries a sense of significance and social status. Some deep-pocketed individuals even declare they need to own these luxuries because as extremely time-poor people they need to have their fast cars and private jets at their disposal anytime they want. I guess that thought process does make sense, but it comes at a huge price.

I'm here to tell you though, you can access many of those assets the wealthy enjoy, but at a fraction of the cost.

I've spent decades trying out many of those luxury toys and am happy to share how I did it so that you can enjoy them too. I'm not going to say it's been a tough life driving some of the world's best supercars, hanging out on super yachts in the sunshine and drinking the finest champagne in first class suites on around-the-world flights, but it was all in the name of research!

While many people are swept up in the detail, I always like to concentrate on the big picture. In the examples outlined in this book, I've ignored things like tax costs, or benefits, and have rounded numbers to things like 50 weeks in the year to make things easier.

Also, rental and mortgage rates have changed over the last few decades so I've included a range of them in my examples. I'd suggest you change the variables as to

If there is a will - there is always a way

what you see fit for now, and for your long term scenario. What might work today (or did in the past) may not work in the future, or even in your neighbourhood. So, carefully consider your individual circumstances before diving in.

Ultimately, my philosophy in life is that if there is a will - there is always a way.

So, dream big and then do whatever it takes to achieve your goals.

CHAPTER 2
WHO IS CHRIS GRAY AND WHY IS IT WORTH LISTENING TO HIM?

I started investing in property at the age of 22, retired from full-time work at Deloitte at the age of 31 and now at 50 years of age (in 2021) I own around $20m worth of real estate.

For over 10 years I've been the host of *Your Property Empire* and other shows on Sky News Business as well as being the real estate expert on *MyHome TV* (Channel 9) and *The Renovators* (Channel 10). I've interviewed and learnt from some of the country's top experts around property and wealth creation. Being both 'inside' the media and 'out in the field', I get to hear the real story rather than what the headlines would have you believe.

Few people have as much 'lifestyle per hour worked' than I do

There are certainly a lot of wealthier people you could listen to, but few people have as much 'lifestyle per hour worked' than I do.

I refer to myself as lazy, but others tell me they see it as efficiency. I worked twice as hard in my twenties so that I could have my thirties and onwards pretty easy. I had a full-time job as an accountant, studied accounting at night school and still had time for socialising and building my property portfolio.

I'm happy being a contrarian

While I am an accountant by trade, I'm not a great technical one. My skill is in reading the numbers and taking the emotion out of decisions, which tends to give me the opposite answer to everyone else. I'm happy being a contrarian, standing out from the crowd and backing my own ideas, rather than following the sheep and the previous generation.

It might seem morbid, but realistically I could die tomorrow, so I don't actually have a bucket list. I live for today, and if I come up with a fun idea, then I implement it straight away.

At Deloitte I was fortunate enough to have a boss who allowed me to start investing in property on the side, as long as my work was done and my internal and external customers were happy. So, I became one of the most efficient people in the office as I knew for every hour I generated, I could spend that extra time doing what I wanted to do.

And I continue to do that now. I often only sleep four to six hours at night, but then I take a 30 to 90-minute nap in the afternoon when my body wants a rest. I work when my body and mind is in the mood and I don't work when it isn't – it just doesn't make any sense to do it any other way.

In 2004, I founded a buyer's agency business called Your Empire where I implement buying homes and investments, just like I would do for myself, but for my clients who want to achieve the same results as I've enjoyed.

We have no office and no staff. Instead, we have self-motivated, self-employed contractors who have a similar outlook as I do. We work together to get results for our clients, and ourselves. There are no clock-watchers, we all know what we need to do, and we do it when and how it suits us.

I want to spend my valuable time with positive people who are keen to learn and are decision makers. If you're a sceptic (who believes you're right and I'm wrong) I'm not here to convert you - so please stop reading now and send this book on to someone more optimistic.

You don't need to agree with all my ideas and suggestions in this book, all I ask is for you to have an open mind and consider a different way of thinking. Take and implement what you enjoy and leave everything else aside or for another day. But for now, thanks for reading and consider paying it forward.

CHAPTER 3
WHERE DO YOU REALLY WANT TO LIVE?

You could live in a house two to three times more expensive than you live in at the moment ... and it could actually cost you less.

Most people can't afford to BUY the property they want in the suburb they want. However, many people could afford to RENT the property they want in the suburb they want.

The problem is, rent money has always been seen as 'dead' money and in Australia there's a social stigma around renting as it supposedly indicates that you are POOR as opposed to RICH.

I'm here to tell you I'm a proud renter

In keeping with my contrarian streak, I'm here to tell you I'm a proud renter - who has been doing it for the last 20 years. I may never own the home I live in again. I learnt long ago that I could afford to rent and live in a property two to three times more expensive than I could afford to buy, so that's what I did.

My accountant at the time said "Sure, renting can be fine now as you're single, but when you get married, life will change". Once that day eventually came, life did change, but it didn't alter my view on renting. He then said "Life will change when you have kids". When that day came too, life did change, but it still didn't alter my view on renting. I then changed accountants. My current accountant is on the same page as me.

Now, I'll explain just how I made this theory work for me, and I'll use Sydney as an example as most people will recognise the suburbs.

If you buy a $1m to $1.5m two-bedroom unit with double bedrooms and parking in a small block close to the water in Bondi Beach, then you should be able to get quite a nice property. If you rent that out at the start of summer on a sunny day (with a savvy property manager) there should be a queue of people wanting to move in - even in a post-pandemic rental market.

So, what happens to the rental price? It goes up because there's a limited supply of available properties and a growing demand – it's the basics of economics. An oversupply of keen tenants is effectively pushing the value up. In 2021, rental yields for these types of units are currently around 3% to 3.5%. That would equate to around $600 to $700 a week on a $1m property.

Let's now take a $3m to $5m property as an alternative, and see how that stacks up as a rental. Well, with $3m to $5m you're going to get a higher quality property in a better street. It is also likely to have superior attributes compared to the $1m property, such as more bedrooms, a pool in the building or grander views.

So, how much would the rent be on that? While it would be more in dollar terms, it will actually be a lot less in percentage terms. Why? Well, how many people could afford the equivalent 3% to 3.5% rent, which would equate to $1800 to $3500 a week? Not nearly as many.

What then happens to the property's rental value? It goes down due to the economics of supply and demand. Rental yields on multimillion-dollar properties can be as low as 1%.

Let's look at the numbers. Here are some of the properties I've rented in the last 20 years - and bear in mind that Sydney rents have generally come down 1% to 1.5% in that time as well so they were even bigger bargains before.

	Value	Weekly rent	Yield
Clovelly	$1.5 million	$620	2.07%
Gordons Bay	$5.9 million	$2,200	1.86%
South Coogee	$6 million	$2,500	2.08%
Double Bay	$6.7 million	$2,500	1.87%
Darling Point	$4.5 million	$1,600	1.78%

Renting as a property investment strategy has become more popular over recent years, especially as property prices continue to rise around the country, making it even harder for people to enter the homeowner market. The concept has been coined 'rentvesting' – renting where you want to live and buying where you can get the best return.

The real return or 'arbitrage' is when you're wanting to rent somewhere with a low yield and then you can invest in properties with a higher yield. Think of it like Monopoly – rent and live in the hotel on Park Lane or Mayfair and then invest in a number of smaller houses in places like Regent St, Bond St, or Leicester Square.

> **'Rentvesting' – renting where you want to live and buying where you can get the best return**

Here's a basic example you can use to see if this method will work for you:

	Investments	Home	Investments	Home
Buy 2 - 4 x $1m investment properties	$2,000,000	$2,000,000	$4,000,000	$4,000,000
Rent money coming in at 3.5%	$70,000		$140,000	
Rent money going out a 2%	($40,000)		($80,000)	
Mortage going out at 3%	($60,000)	($60,000)	($120,000)	($120,000)
Rental / mortage cost	($30,000)	($60,000)	($60,000)	($120,000)
Saving / year	$30,000		$60,000	
Saving / week	$600		$1,200	

Back in 2009, I rented a place in Double Bay right on the water and the numbers looked like this:

	Investments	Home
Purchase	6.7 x $1m	$6,700,000
Mortage 7%	**($470,000)**	**($470,000)**
Rent In 4.5%	$300,000	$0
Tax back 33%	$55,000	
Rent Out $2,500/wk	**($125,000)**	
Total Cost	**($240,000)**	**($470,000)**

So, I was saving about $230,000 by renting.

This example shows you how you could buy three $1m properties (instead of a $3m home) and then rent a $6m place instead:

	Investments	Home
Purchase	3 x $1m	$3,000,000
Mortage 3.00%	**($90,000)**	**($90,000)**
Rent In 3.50%	$105,000	
Rent Out 1.75%	**$105,000**	
Total Cost	**($90,000)**	**($90,000)**
Rental property value	$6,000,000	

Remember to always check your numbers with suitably qualified mortgage brokers, accountants and financial planners before making a financial decision as these numbers will change depending on the property, location and year you do it. Ideally, try and find advisers who understand these concepts as many don't, and will concentrate on trying to save you $1 rather than make you $2.

You can then use those extra savings to:

☑ Buy more property

☑ Rent a better property

☑ Pay down your mortgages

☑ Invest in other assets

☑ Have more fun

☑ Or all of the above

The benefits I get from 'rentvesting' include the following:

- I buy median priced investments in 'blue chip' suburbs as they are more stable and less volatile when markets move quickly. I can easily sell one or two if I need to, no matter what the market conditions. Expensive properties can take years to sell and can drop by massive amounts if you're a forced seller

- By purchasing properties with low strata fees I avoid the associated costs of expensive lifts, gyms and pools. Some of the properties on the market today have strata fees in the region of $50,000 to $100,000 per unit each year. So instead of getting a 2% return, owners of such properties may only be getting 1%.

- As all of my debt is against investment properties, then it is all deductible. Whereas, any debt on my family home is non-deductible. Sure, my properties aren't free of capital gains tax, but if I never sell then I never pay the tax. I can still extract the equity by refinancing (see my other book for more details: *The Effortless Empire - The time-poor professional's guide to building wealth from property* can be downloaded for FREE at **www.yourempire.com.au/bonus**)

- Part of the cost of renting our home can be offset against our household income as my wife and I have a home office to work from. If you did this at your own home, it would affect part of the capital gains-free allowance.

When I evaluate which steps to take in life, I always try and look at the big picture and therefore I don't take everything down to the dollars and cents. Often things can change, such as tax laws, so I don't want one change in the environment to suddenly force me to change my strategy. That is why I think of those benefits as 'added extras' rather than the main reasons for doing the things I do.

Over the years I've been asked several questions about my property investment strategy and here are some of the answers to the most common queries.

ISN'T RENT MONEY STILL DEAD MONEY?

Only if you don't invest the equivalent money elsewhere into either property, shares or business.

WILL THIS STRATEGY WORK EVERYWHERE?

No. You need to work out the comparative rental yields on local properties you want to live in and then compare that to properties you can afford to invest in. If there's a big difference, then it COULD work for you.

We also decided to upgrade homes every time we move so then it's a positive step and a new adventure

WHY WOULD SOMEONE RENT OUT AN EXPENSIVE PROPERTY FOR SUCH A LOW YIELD?

Often, they have previously lived in it as a family home and they've held onto it rather than pay the high cost of selling and re-buying elsewhere. Or, they've moved overseas and think they'll return later on. Some owners may have completely paid off their mortgage so as long as the rent covers the maintenance, strata fees and land tax - they're happy to rent it out.

AREN'T YOU WORRIED ABOUT BEING KICKED OUT EVERY 12 MONTHS?

Yes, we used to and then rather than dread it all year we got into the mindset of assuming we're going to move. Then, if we get the option to stay it's a bonus. We also decided to upgrade homes every time we move so then it's a positive step and a new adventure. Since we've changed our mindset, we haven't moved in the last 10 years.

ISN'T IT A HASSLE AND STRESSFUL MOVING OFTEN?

Sure, it can be, so we go on holidays instead. We pay a removalist to come in after we've left, they pack up the house, move it, unpack it at the other end and then the cleaner comes in and makes the beds. That's 80% of the hard work done so we just need to polish the last 20%.

BUT DOESN'T IT BOTHER YOU THAT YOU CAN'T RENOVATE TO YOUR OWN TASTE?

Actually, you often can make changes if you ask permission, use professional tradespeople, are improving the property, or offer up an additional bond and/or guarantee that you'll put it back the way you found it.

HOW DO YOU CONVINCE YOUR PARTNER?

Show them what you can afford to RENT and then what you can afford to BUY – if the difference is big enough, it should be a no-brainer.

IS IT WORTH FORCING YOUR PARTNER TO RENT?

No. A divorce will cost you more!

IS THIS FOR EVERYONE?

No. It's for people who embrace change and WANT it to work.

Anytime you have questions or comments, feel free to email me at: **chris.gray@yourempire.com.au**

HOW ABOUT MORE FREE RESOURCES?

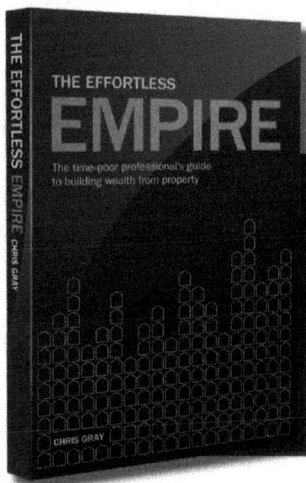

WANT MORE?

THE EFFORTLESS
EMPIRE
The time-poor professional's guide
to building wealth from property

CHRIS GRAY

Get Chris Gray's book
**"The Effortless Empire
- The time-poor
professional's guide
to building wealth
from property"**

and Chris will share even more of his contrarian tips, tricks and ideas with his regular emails.

www.yourempire.com.au/bonus

CHAPTER 4
HOW TO GET BEHIND THE WHEEL OF YOUR DREAM CAR

CAN A LAMBORGHINI REALLY BE CHEAPER THAN A BMW OR MERCEDES?

I grew up in the UK, where you could always tell who was 'wealthy' and had a brand-new car because each year the registration plates started with the next letter of the alphabet. In 1983 it was A, then B in 1984, and so on. Now they have the year eg. 20 for a car produced in 2020. Even people with private number plates would often get their car delivered with the manufacturer's plates to start with, just to show off to their neighbours that they can afford a brand-new car.

Depreciation costs a lot of money

Although that fancy new car smell (and the chance to show off a little) might be tempting, it's common knowledge that brand new cars depreciate the minute you drive them off the lot. It's easy to justify a new car though by saying "I get three to five years' warranty with the car" or "I salary sacrifice my car so it's more tax efficient". These days you might get an instant asset write off with a purchase. No matter how you want to justify it to your husband, wife, accountant, mate or neighbour - depreciation costs a lot of money.

I would rather put that depreciation into buying a better car (not a newer one) as most people don't know that much about cars to realise which is the current model. And in Australia we don't have the number plate suffix as a giveaway. Even if people do know you're driving a secondhand car, who cares what they think anyway?

At 24 years old, I was fortunate enough to buy a secondhand bright red 1986 Porsche 911 GTS. To me it looked a million dollars and it was any schoolboy's dream car. I didn't care that it was nine years old – it was a Porsche, and I was 24! It still drove as fast as when it was a brand-new car.

I paid about £12,000 for the Porsche and sold it just over two years later for £10,500, which then funded my seven-month world trip and adventures when I emigrated to Australia at 27. If I had bought a brand-new car for £12,000, the proceeds might have only given me a one-to-two-month holiday.

Bringing that up to current day numbers, in Australia we pay a fortune in luxury car tax and if you want a brand new Ferrari, Lamborghini, Bentley or Rolls Royce, it's going to cost you a pretty penny. Then, a lot of that value is going to be lost within the first week.

In December 2012, I bought a 2005 Lamborghini Murcielago Roadster in bright orange for $250,000 with 23,695 kilometres on the clock. I believe the brand new list price, on road with options, was around $750,000 at the time.

Being in the property industry, I see most of the real estate agents run around in the latest greatest BMW or Mercedes cars which could range in cost from $100,000 to more than $300,000. So, for the same money, I could have bought a brand new $250,000 car, or drive a second hand $750,000 car for half the yearly cost of interest and depreciation.

To make a true like-for-like comparison you would need to add in servicing (and believe me, you know what a service bill is when you receive one on a Lamborghini). A clutch can be $10,000 to $15,000 and if you drive it regularly, but respectfully, you might need one every two to three years. Drive it like you stole it and the clutch can be done in an hour!

I estimate my yearly cost of insuring and maintaining the Lamborghini was $10,000 to $15,000 so it still worked out cheaper than driving away with (and maintaining) a shiny new sports car.

	Lamborghni	Lamborghni	BMW / Mercedes
	2005	New	New
Car cost	$250,000	$750,000	$250,000
Depreciation	$10,000	$150,000	$40,000
Interest @ 7%	$17,500	$52,500	$17,500
Cost / year	$27,500	$202,500	$57,500

Despite loving driving cars, trucks, boats and any other toy I can get my hands on, I actually know nothing about them mechanically or performance-wise. So, I joined the Lamborghini Club of NSW to learn more and to go on weekend drives. No one cared that I turned up in a seven-year-old car as most of the members weren't high-flying yuppies or stockbrokers from the city. Some had saved up their whole life to buy their dream car and knew every nut, bolt and difference between all the makes and models. No matter what your background, or whether you drove a

$100,000 to $200,000 model or the latest $1m plus Aventador SV. Everyone appreciated the different cars for what they were.

A year later, one of the members said to me "You know your car has probably appreciated $100,000 in the last year and is probably worth over $350,000 now?". I knew secondhand cars didn't depreciate by as much as brand new cars, but I hadn't ever experienced an appreciating car.

Your car has probably appreciated $100,000

My insurance policy was up for renewal and I saw I had an agreed value on the car of $250,000, so I rang my insurer and said I believe my agreed value might be out of date and could they review it before I renew. Three days later they confirmed is was worth $350,000. The naysayers would probably argue that comes with an increase in premium, but who cares if you pay more for insurance if you've just made $100,000?

A few years later, I felt like it was time for a change, so I looked for the next model up - a Lamborghini Murcielago SV - which to the naked eye seems like exactly the same car, but it is slightly faster. However, not only would I have had the hassle of trying to sell my current model, then I would have the added cost of paying more for another car, while hoping it had been well looked after, and then have to pay about $10,000 in stamp duty.

So, what did I do? I wrapped my existing car in chrome purple, and it felt like a brand new car - without the hassle (and expense) of actually buying one. Car wraps are becoming more popular these days and it's almost impossible to tell the difference on a complete colour change (unless you get very close). They range in price from around $5,000 to $10,000

depending on the material used and the design you choose. Chrome was a lot more expensive (as it's very reflective and shows up any blemishes) therefore it needs a clear wrap on top to make sure it doesn't scratch.

SO WHAT'S THE DOWNSIDE OF OWNING A SUPERCAR?

While the Lamborghini tale is a great story, not every day is glamorous when you own a car that is worth more than some people's houses.

It might be a car I bought for $250,000, but it's still essentially a $750,000 car and it tends to come with 750,000 problems! The worst service I had was around $30,000. I had a clutch go but while they had the engine out, they found another $10,000 issue. So, as well as finding the money to buy the car in the first place, you need to have a cash buffer - just like you would with a property - to maintain it. There's no point having a luxury car if it sits in the garage because you can't afford the fuel or a service on it.

THEY CAN DRIVE YOU CRAZY

In 2018, I was driving along the M4 with my wife and something felt wrong with the handling so I pulled over. As it turned out, all the nuts had come loose on the rear passenger side wheel and we almost lost it at 100kph. Everything was fine, but it did cost $10,000 to repair and replace the wheel and hub. Insurance covered it, but I still had to pay an excess of $2,500.

During the same year I got some dents and scrapes to the side of the car, although I didn't notice straight away as it was the passenger side. Believe me, it's not cheap to re-spray a Lamborghini and to match all the panels (around $40,000). Again, luckily the insurance covered it, but it could have been my cost if I hadn't been adequately insured.

With the car then in pristine condition, I decided to sell after owning it for about seven years. I wasn't driving it as much because I had purchased a couple of other cars. It was now a 14-year-old car with 66,000 kms on it – one of the highest mileage Lamborghinis in the country. It was also bright orange, and then purple chrome, which isn't everyone's cup of tea as many people want to travel under the radar and not let their customers (and employees) know how they're doing financially. A convertible roadster stands out like a sore thumb too compared to a hard top coupe, and it was automatic rather than manual.

By the end of 2018, beginning of 2019, it was the credit crunch, when no one was lending money, so the luxury car market crashed. My $350,000 agreed value was looking more like $250,000, and that's if I could find a buyer.

I owned a supercar for seven years, drove over 40,000 kms in it and sold it for a $40,000 profit during COVID!

In the end, it took me about 15 months to sell. I had about six enquiries who never even answered my messages, a couple who low-balled me, but I eventually sold it in the week COVID-19 hit Australia to a person who just loved it and paid $290,000 on a $297,000 sale price.

The pros of my Lamborghini ownership:

- Driving a secondhand $750,000 car instead of a brand new $250,000 one

- It's got a Lamborghini badge for a reason – the acceleration is similar to a jet fighter plane

- I could still drive it to its true potential – there are plenty of racetracks with driver training days

- They can still be everyday cars – mine had child seats to take the kids to kindergarten, space for the golf clubs and it got me to and from the local shopping centre

- I owned a supercar for seven years, drove over 40,000 kms in it and sold it for a $40,000 profit during COVID!

The cons of my Lamborghini ownership:

- A secondhand $750,000 car costs more to insure (and repair) than a brand new $250,000 alternative

- They can take a very long time to sell, so you never want to be a desperate seller

- You need to treat such cars with respect as they are old

So far, my car ownership history has included a Porsche 911 GTS, Ferrari Mondial, Ferrari 355 GTS and a Ferrari 360 Spyder. Since selling my Lamborghini Murcielago the next natural move would be to a Lamborghini Aventador Roadster, but that comes at a cost of more than $1m brand new or around

$500,000 to $600,000 for a secondhand one - and that's a lot of money.

When you buy your first supercar, you'll drive it every day for years. After having a number of them for decades, the thrill does wear off slightly so now I'm thinking my strategy needs to change.

More expensive, doesn't always mean more fun

Read the following chapter of this book for my next plan.

In the meantime, I'm now really into the old classics – they're just as much fun, but a different kind of entertainment for (usually) less financial outlay. However, there can be even more in yearly outgoings depending on how rare your vintage wheels are. Ultimately, once you don't care what people think, it doesn't really matter what you drive and you'll soon realise that more expensive, doesn't always mean more fun.

HERE'S WHAT'S CURRENTLY IN MY GARAGE

1912 Ford Model T

- The first original mass-produced car over 100 years ago with 15 million cars made!

- I thought these cars would be worth more than $500,000 but in fact it was only $32,000 as there are still supposedly 1 million in circulation

- Super simple mechanics with hardly any electrics and gravitational fuel, but it can be a nightmare to find someone to work on them

- A death trap on wheels – no seat belts and skinny wheels equals poor stopping, especially in the wet

- Amazing fun though, and I always wanted to own a car with a crank handle after watching Chitty Chitty Bang Bang

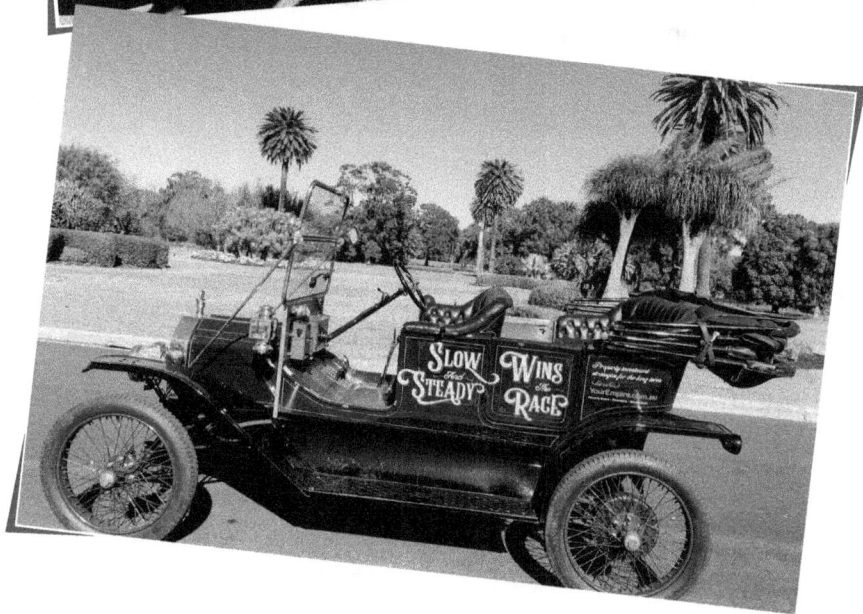

1985 Cadillac Stretch Limousine

- Now converted into a rally car for doing charity races with Mystery Box Rally, which is part of the Shitbox Rally Challenge. Find out more on **www.boxrallies.com**

- Completely impractical and everyone said it wouldn't make it, but it did on the third attempt

- It only cost $22,000, but I have spent over $100,000 on repairs and maintenance – so it turned out to be much more expensive than owning a Lamborghini

- You only live once and this is great fun, a great way to see the Australia that not many people get to see and an amazing way to raise money and support local farmers and communities

1969 Ford Econoline Van

- Why would I buy a van? Because I can. Plus, I was bored in lockdown during COVID

- Despite being mechanically checked over, my $20,000 COVID impulse purchase has turned into a $60,000 to $70,000 van with a brand-new Ford Racing engine, front racing seats and a rear leather bench seat that converts to a queen size flat bed

- Possibly the most expensive camp bed I have ever spent a night on

- It's one of a kind, a real head turner and I'm loving every minute of it

These cars are great fun to own but don't cost a fortune. If I wanted to buy some other classic, vintage or veteran cars that were a limited edition they would cost me millions. Buying cheaper versions means I can have more fun and not care where I park them.

DEPRECIATING ASSETS

Should they be leased, or paid for in cash?

When I was 30 and working at Deloitte, I tried to salary sacrifice a Ferrari 355, but I worked out the fringe benefits tax on it would have been more than my $80,000 wage. The tax was calculated on the list price of the car when it was new, not on what I had paid for it. The car had cost about $450,000 when new, but (as usual) I bought a secondhand one for about $200,000.

I got a 100% lease to purchase it, a move which caused a lot of comments from my colleagues. "You should only pay for a depreciating asset in cash when you can afford it," they said. I had other ideas.

I could pay for the car in cash and then I would own a $200,000 depreciating Ferrari with no debt. Or, I could borrow $200,000 secured against the car and then use that sum to buy a $1m investment property, by putting down a 20% deposit ($200,000) and getting a $800,000 mortgage. If that property rose at 5% to 10% then I would make $50,000 to $100,000 a year which would more than offset the interest costs on the car lease.

I believe that's a good strategy from a property investment perspective when your limiting factor for building a bigger portfolio is having a deposit.

Years later, when I went to buy the Lamborghini, I had enough of a deposit but my limiting factor was serviceability. Instead of getting a car loan for $250,000, I borrowed $250,000 against one of my properties (with a different split loan account so I could separate deductible and non-deductible debt).

Repayments on a $250,000 car loan would have been around $4,000 a month or $50,000 a year, whereas those same repayments could be used to service an extra $1m mortgage. So, it made more financial sense to use my portfolio

You need to be surrounded by experts and advisers

equity to pay for the car so I could then buy another property. Also, the interest rate on a loan secured against a property was probably about half the rate of a car loan.

So hopefully you can see that your finance strategy for paying for properties, cars, boats and other assets will change over time depending on your life stage, your attitude to risk, and the banks' lending criteria. This is why you need to be surrounded by experts and advisers who understand the whole picture.

A good adviser might save you a few thousand dollars in tax. A great adviser could guide you to buy an additional property, the profits of which could then pay for a 'free' Ferrari or Lamborghini, plus extra money left over.

FROM SUPERCARS, TO LUXURY CARS AND TRACK CARS

It's one thing to be wealthy and own one supercar, but what about owning a whole collection? That would certainly take a few million dollars, a very, very large garage and impeccable security.

Is this really possible if you aren't a multi-millionaire? Of course it is. You just need to think outside the box.

Why pay for a supercar every day if you don't drive it every day?

Back in 2007, I decided to sell my Ferrari 355 GTS as I had had it for a number of years and was at the time thinking about getting into rally driving. However, I wasn't sure which supercar to get next – I was keen on a Lamborghini but wasn't sure I could deal with (or afford) the unreliability and associated expenses.

So, I took the alternative route and decided to buy a Mitsubishi Evo 9 as a day-to-day car and then join a supercar club.

The concept is similar to the boat syndicates but with added extras:

- Why pay for a supercar every day if you don't drive it every day?

- Why stick with one supercar when you often need a different one for different occasions?

It made a lot of sense – it was great fun to drive a Hummer, but it was difficult to get it into a Westfield car park. A Lamborghini was amazing on a summer's day, but not so great if you've got a family day out with two kids. The Bentley Arnage was a fantastic luxury cruiser, but not so good on a sporty drive day in the country, or on a racetrack.

In the club I joined, there were three levels of membership and you received a certain amount of points for an annual fee. With around 10 to 20 cars in the fleet, each vehicle had varying levels of points depending on when you wanted to use them. So, a Lamborghini at the weekend in summer could be as high as 60 points, but a Hummer during the week in winter could be just two points.

With each membership you were allowed to name a husband and wife as drivers on the policy. So, I thought, why not join with a mate and split the membership as then we would get a cheaper cost per car. We joined as husband and 'wife' and paid $18,250 for 500 points each (I'm still not sure who was the husband and who was the wife).

	Annual Membership	Points Allowance	Per Point
Membership 1	$36,500	1,000	$37
Membership 2	$32,000	750	$43
Membership 3	$27,000	550	$49

My mate (or 'wife') and I chose to use most of the cars during the week as we both had flexible working hours. That way, the cars 'cost' about a third of the points. Effectively, we got to use three times as many cars during the week than we would have at the weekend. During weekdays there were also less people on the road, so it was more fun to drive them anyway.

From memory, I got to use a car for about 60 days, or five days per month, which equates to around $300 a car per day. That's a very cheap way of having a fleet of 10 to 20 cars at your disposal, compared to shelling out millions of dollars - and also having the hassle (and cost) of maintaining them.

The pros of belonging to a supercar club:

- Having a fleet of cars for a variety of uses you may have for different occasions

- Getting sparkling clean cars delivered to your door

- No maintenance issues

- Having an inexpensive way to test drive multiple expensive cars

- Experiencing the cars change over time to keep the interest of members

The cons of belonging to a supercar club:

- You need to book in advance and can't use them whenever you want - especially at short notice

- You don't have any choice in the fleet of cars on offer

Unfortunately, this type of car club isn't available any more in Australia, as far as I'm aware. There used to be one for classic cars, however it only lasted a few years. Overseas these clubs are very popular, especially in London. I'm not sure why, but I think it might be because there are lots of 'flash Harrys' in the UK who are happy to flaunt their wealth. I think Australia's Tall Poppy Syndrome means many people like to stay under the radar and perhaps prefer to own a single car in a dark colour just to drive on a Sunday morning. It's a shame, I hope these types of clubs do re-appear down under.

If the idea sounds good to you, why not get a few mates together and set up one yourself, just like I did with my initial boat syndicate? (Jump to the next chapter to find out more.)

GLOBETROTTING BEHIND THE WHEEL OF A SUPERCAR

The next stage in my car driving journey is to do a series of weeks away where you get to try out a range of supercars in a foreign country while meeting new people and having a five-to-six-star hotel experience.

The cost of an international road trip can range from around $15,000 to $30,000 a week, depending on the amount of drive days, the variety of cars, and whether you want to stay in a luxury suite or are happy to twin share in a five-star room. Experiences range from ice driving in Scandinavia, staying on a super yacht during the Monaco Grand Prix, attending the Goodwood Festival of Speed, experiencing track days at Nürburgring, or racing around France, Germany, Italy and Switzerland.

The tour cars include:

- ☑ Audi R8 V10
- ☑ Bentley Continental GT
- ☑ Chevrolet Corvette Z06
- ☑ Dodge Viper
- ☑ Ferrari 488 GTB
- ☑ Ferrari 812 Superfast
- ☑ Lamborghini Aventador
- ☑ Lamborghini Huracan

☑   McLaren 720S

☑   Mercedes AMG GT

☑   Porsche 911 GT3

These aren't cheap days that everyone can afford, but they are certainly a lot less expensive than the cost of owning a collection of these cars. And the best part is - you haven't got the risk and hassle of maintenance and repairs as long as you treat them with respect.

An experience like this should be cheaper than hiring a car directly, and since organisers drive a lead and a follow up car then there's a limit of how badly people can treat the cars. You normally get a good bunch of like-minded people at these events and there is usually a 'no d*ck head policy'.

Compare this to a hire car company giving a stranger the keys for a week and just crossing their fingers that they're not going to abuse the cars by shredding the tyres and burning the clutch as soon as they turn the corner. Insurance excess costs for rentals can be as high as $10,000 to $30,000 and I don't like your chances of getting it back.

In Australia, some of these drive day experiences can cost between $2,000 and $4,000 a day (including lunch at a fine restaurant, of course).

HITTING THE RACETRACK IN A SUPERCAR

One of the pleasures of owning a supercar is being able to experience driving well in excess of the speed limit in the safe confines of a racetrack, of which there are several dotted around Australia. Most car clubs (Porsche, Ferrari, Lamborghini) run their own events and there are a number of private companies that run public and private days as well. Instructors are usually on hand to help out virgin track drivers and to show individuals how to drive their car faster, and safer. If you get them to drive your car, then you'll quickly see why they are called supercars and may even discover that they can go round corners at probably twice the speed you previously thought – it all comes down to the driver.

I've been driving on racetracks since I was 24 and while I would like to think my driving skills have improved in the 25 plus years since, I think I'm probably getting slower and more cautious with age. I never thought I would risk crashing a £12,000 Porsche 911, but then I moved to a $90,000 Ferrari Mondial, a $200,000 Ferrari 355 and then a $250,000 Lamborghini. Before you know it, you're risking a lot of money.

I have had my rear wheel come off and overtake me at 100kph

I've never had any crashes, but I have had my rear wheel come off and overtake me at 100kph while going around a corner. I recently took my wife's Audi RS4 wagon to the skid pan and broke it after two minutes – sometimes the modern cars freak out and go into shutdown mode when you get them to do something out of the ordinary. It wasn't the $8,000 repair bill that was the biggest issue, it was her not having a car over Christmas that was more painful! Lucky we were in partial COVID lockdown and we weren't using it that much anyway.

If I were to buy a Lamborghini Aventador Roadster for $500,000 to $1m, then I would have to slow down as usually these cars aren't even insured on the track. So, my alternative plan is to spend more days driving the racetrack's cars while literally test-driving a whole range of vehicles, with none of the liability.

Mercedes does a half drive day at various tracks for $1,250 (at the time of going to press) in their super-fast AMG models. The instructors let you drive as fast as your ability will let you (which could cost Mercedes more than double in wear and tear on those vehicles) so that potential customers can fully experience their cars - and eventually buy one. BMW offers a similar day.

Audi does an R8 day for around $3,500 with full track analysis, one-on-one personal coaching, full Grand Prix track lapping plus a lapping debrief and analysis.

At other tracks you can drive a race-prepared Mazda MX5, Toyota 86, Golf GTI, Porsche 911 or a Radical SR3 which is like a genuine race car. Prices range from $500 a day, to a few thousand dollars.

During these track days, because you have instructors in the cars with you, the insurance excess isn't extreme and the chance of crashing (and causing serious damage or injury) is vastly reduced. Compare that to the cost of you owning your own race-prepared car or risking your daily driver and you're miles ahead.

YOU COULD ALWAYS RENT BEFORE YOU BUY

Another option for fine car aficionados is just to rent a luxury car by the hour, sit in the back seat and relax.

One car on my wish list is a Rolls Royce Phantom as I love the prestige and styling of the British classic. After selling my Lamborghini, I went on some test drives and tried out the Cullinan, Wraith, Ghost and Phantom. While all great cars, I loved the 'crusie-ability' of the Phantom as opposed to the sportiness of the Wraith.

Although a new Rolls with all the options is over $1m brand new, you can still buy a 2007 or 2008 model for around $200,000 to $300,000. Again, why pay for $700,000 of depreciation just to have a shiny new one? A secondhand Rolls might only have 10,000 to 20,000 kms on the clock and might have been chauffeur-driven just a couple of kilometres a few times a week.

While $200,000 to $300,000 is a 'bargain' compared to the more than $1m price tag of a new Rolls, it's still a significant sum and yet another car to garage, register and maintain. But I think I've found an alternative way to get behind the wheel of a Rolls for a year or two – let's call it a 'try before you buy'.

There are plenty of Ghosts and Phantoms rolling around at the weekend as wedding cars, but often they're just sitting around during the week. So, for $200 to $300 an hour, with a minimum two-hour hire, you can actually use one to chauffeur you around.

Do that twice a month and you would only be up for $10,000 a year – probably the same price you would pay for the registration, maintenance and insurance of a Rolls - without having to pay the upfront capital cost.

This year, I turn 50, so the plan is to experience a Rolls for some of my events with family and friends and see how I enjoy the ride. Who knows, a Rolls Royce might be next on my luxury car list.

RESOURCES - SUPERCAR DRIVING TOURS

I met Anthony Moss and Julie Hunter about 10 years ago and it is now on the top of my bucket list to experience one of their luxury driving tours every other year, if not every year, from now on. They run them in Europe, USA and Australia.

Considering most Supercar owners will be lucky to do 2,000 – 3,000 kms in a year, you will drive nearly half that distance for a fraction of the cost to own one, on roads the cars were made for, and then park it outside a very nice hotel and just leave the keys inside as you take a glass of champagne and get ready for dinner. The next morning the cars are washed and valeted, then you can jump back behind the wheel of another amazing vehicle to enjoy.

www.ultimatedrivingtours.com

HOW ABOUT MORE FREE RESOURCES?

CHAPTER 5
SO, YOU FANCY OWNING A BOAT?

You've surely heard the following saying, which is probably true for many boat owners.

The greatest lesson I have learnt from more than 20 years of boat ownership is – if you don't use something every day, why pay for it every day?

When I first came to Australia in 1997, I got offered a third share in a boat for $3,000 with two new friends. You can probably imagine the quality of speedboat we had when it was worth just $9,000.

"The two happiest days in a boat owner's life are the day you buy the boat, and the day you sell the boat."

It was a piece of rubbish, but I was a boat owner and I loved it. Sure, it broke down all the time, but I had come from the UK where no one owned a boat. That feeling of cruising under the Sydney Harbour Bridge was unbelievable.

A few years on, we were all earning more money and the boat was becoming more and more unreliable, so we bought a brand new $50,000 Haynes Signature. It was still nothing special, but it smelt new and was certainly more luxurious than the last one - plus it was under warranty.

Although there were three of us in the syndicate, our boat spent plenty of time floating on the mooring unused. So,

If you don't use something every day, why pay for it every day?

we thought why not have eight of us? Then the boat would only cost $7,000 each and $150 a month each to cover mooring, maintenance and other miscellaneous costs. With eight of us in the syndicate we would still get to use it every other weekend for half a day each, which was often more than enough on a sunny day as there wasn't a roof on the boat.

The plan worked like a dream and it was cheap boating. I got off work early during the week, swam out to the swing mooring at Balmoral and then drove it out to the Opera House steps to pick up my colleagues for a cruise and a drink. The only downside was swimming back in from the swing mooring to the beach - especially at shark feeding time.

Three years later, we were all earning more money (although we were far from being millionaires earning around $80,000 a year each) and had dreams of getting an even better boat. The day came when we got a $100,000 23ft Sea Ray. After selling the Haines Signature for $25,000, we got back half of what we spent to purchase it, so it only meant tipping in another $10,000 each.

To me, this is affordable boating at a reasonable price. Depreciation was $2,000 to $3,000 a year and $1,000 to $2,000 a year for expenses. At first everyone is trying to use the boat every day, but like most things the novelty wears off after a while, especially in winter. As time passed, I found I was getting to use the boat whenever I wanted.

The day finally came when one of the syndicate members took things to a whole other level. If we could make a syndicate work on a $100,000 boat, why couldn't it work on a $1m to $2m boat? Well, it did work, and he set up a whole business around it - owning more than a dozen boats at any one time.

By then I was in my forties with young kids who got seasick bouncing around on a little speedboat and I was also wanting to entertain a lot of our corporate clients, advisers and referral partners. So, we started off on a $1m 45-foot Absolute Flybridge which could host 18 people, had three bedrooms on the lower level, a kitchen and lounge on the mid-level, and an outdoor table and sun loungers on the upper level. It was a great family boat - and an even better entertainer.

An eighth share was $130,000 and it cost me $1,200 a month for ongoing expenses. The deal was 'walk on, walk off' which meant I didn't have to clean or tidy the boat, it was all done for us. Better still, it was pristine every time we jumped on, just like a floating hotel room.

The syndicate members owned the boat, and the management company did all the maintenance. It was to be owned for three and a half years and then sold, ideally for 50% to 60% of it's original value. That way, it would still be in warranty for major cost minimisation and it would always be looking like a million dollars.

I've crunched the numbers below to show that an eighth share in a $1m boat is not as unaffordable as one might think, only $43,500 rather than the $345,200 it might cost you to own it.

Sure, being part of a syndicate meant we had to follow some rules, mainly the booking system, and we couldn't necessarily use it whenever we wanted. But really, how much do boat owners actually use their boats anyway?

In our syndicate system, each member had 43 days each (multiply that by eight and that's 344 days, with 21 days left for maintenance). Of that time you could have three bookings of up to three days each at any time, and when it came to major boat-friendly days like New Year's Eve and Australia Day, names were drawn out of a hat. Also, if no one was using the boat tomorrow, you could book it as a standby date, which meant that day didn't come out of your 43 days - all you had to do was pay a $200 cleaning fee.

Life comes first, work comes second

I was probably one of the few in the syndicate who used my full 43 days (plus some standby days) every year. I've worked from home for years and I'm fortunate enough to have a pretty relaxed 'job' - I designed it that way myself. Life comes first, work comes second, and the majority of my income and wealth comes from my pretty passive property portfolio. It would take me just 30 minutes a month to oversee.

Technically, my 'job' is to go out, meet people and spread the word of my property investing philosophies. The more I travel, drive head-turning cars and hang out on luxury boats, the more people ask, "How do you do it?" That's when I share my story and introduce them to the strategies that have worked for me. Rather than spending hours explaining these strategies to every potential customer, I wrote my first book *The Effortless Empire: The time-poor professional's guide to building wealth from property*. You can find it for free at **www.yourempire.com.au/bonus**. If people like what they read, then my team and I can implement it for them.

Nowadays, I mainly use the boat during the week either as a floating office or to take out other businesspeople who have flexible jobs too. An old adage says that you build a certain relationship with a one-hour coffee meeting, but you build an even stronger one with a four-hour game of golf. Imagine the kind of professional relationship you can build when you spend eight to ten hours on a luxury boat?

Imagine the kind of professional relationship you can build when you spend eight to ten hours on a luxury boat?

When owning a syndicate boat works for you:

☑   If you have flexibility in your work or leisure time

☑   If you can make plans in advance

☑   If you have a positive attitude and can go with the flow

It's not going to work for you when:

☑   You love doing things last minute with no prior notice

☑   You are embarrassed to admit that you don't own your own boat

While the cost of a boat is NOT tax deductible (even though you may be entertaining staff, clients and referral partners) I still found my business got the upside in having one at my disposal. Having it for friends and family to use as well, that was a bonus.

If $43,500 a year is still too much to justify, but you still would like part-time ownership of a boat, then there's always another way. Why not buy the share with a mate who you enjoy spending time with (and would probably be on the boat with anyway)? Suddenly, the cost has halved to just over $20,000.

After a year of sharing the 45-foot Absolute Flybridge, we upgraded to a 52-foot Absolute Flybridge as it gave us more space for corporate entertaining. The cost for an eighth share was $200,000 for a $1.6m boat. Four of us are now looking at getting into an eighth share on a $2m boat, which would be $250,000 or $62,500 each.

If getting into a boat share, or syndicate, interests you there are two main types to consider. Ours was one where we paid for the capital cost of the boat, which were always brand new. Technically, this should be the cheapest way as we own the boat with no debt so the management company doesn't need to pay for high interest costs. Their main risk, however, is to be able to sell all eight shares. This system is great if members have the capital to put down and are happy to commit for a fixed period. Members can often sell before the end of that term, if there's someone interested in getting in. The downside of this model is putting the capital down up front and not knowing the ongoing costs, or what price the boat will sell for after the time period.

Another scenario is paying a yearly fee in return for a set number of points, or days on the boat. The company running it then has to buy and finance the boats and that cost generally gets passed on to the members with a profit element on top. It's for this reason these companies often buy secondhand boats which are a lot cheaper upfront. The advantage is however, you don't need a big capital outlay to get in and you can often just sign up for a one-year minimum. The downside is you're on an older boat, which isn't as impressive, and it might break down more often.

There can be other costs that need to be accounted for with a boat share. You will need to also budget for fuel, a skipper (and wait staff for bigger boats and corporate entertaining), plus alcohol and food. If you've got nice friends, then it's easy to make your boat days out a BYO affair, but not many people will offer to fill a boat up at the fuel bowser – if they do it once, then they probably wouldn't do it again. Filling the tank on a big boat isn't cheap, especially if you've been driving it around like a speedboat! If you're cruising though, it might only be $500 to $1,000 for a good day out.

FLOATING THE IDEA OF BOAT RENTAL VERSUS A BOAT SYNDICATE?

Before you commit and dive into an expensive big boat syndicate, consider testing the waters by renting a boat. You can get some great boats for around $500 an hour with a four-hour minimum that will fit more than 20 guests. While some of them may be old, once you're onboard, it's often the view that you're looking at, not the interiors.

At the end of the day, having access to a luxury boat is a great lifestyle accessory and owning one can be addictive. Just be aware that it is often also an expensive past time you're forever trying to upgrade.

SO WHAT'S SO SUPER ABOUT A SUPER YACHT?

Cruising around in a $1m to $2m boat is great fun and I love it. But there's always someone just across the water with a bigger and more expensive boat. These are the super yachts.

A super yacht is commonly described as a commercially-operated luxury yacht (motor or sail powered), which is professionally crewed and has a load line length of 80 feet (24 metres) or more.

The major difference between luxury yachts is size. While a super yacht is deemed to be anything above 80 feet, a mega yacht refers to anything above 200 feet (60 metres).

If you go from a 45-foot boat to a 52-foot boat, it might be 15% longer, but it's not 15% more space or 15% more expensive. It is simply longer, wider and higher. Our 45-foot boat was $1m, whereas our 52-foot boat was $1.6m.

Once you get into super yachts and mega yachts territory, the numbers will blow you out of the water. They start incredibly high at $5m to $10m and get into the tens - and hundreds - of millions of dollars. Owners often say you need to budget 10% of the cost of a boat for expenses and just like the cars, it's 10% of the cost at new - not the secondhand price you might have paid. Realistically, the secondhand boat would cost even more to maintain.

You can drive a 52-foot boat single-handed, especially if you're driving from the top deck where you have 360-degree vision and the boat has the latest bow thruster technology.

It's a different situation on a super yacht where you'll need a team including a full-time captain, engineer, deckhand and probably wait staff. All that comes at an impressive cost.

So how do you afford to hang out on a super yacht? Well for me, this would definitely be a rental opportunity and definitely not a liability that I would want to own. One bad day could cost me my whole property portfolio.

About 10 years ago, I met a guy at a networking event who manages super yachts. I don't know if he knew it, but he and I became 'best friends' overnight! He gave me the lowdown on the uber luxury boats and I soon after booked one for a Christmas party.

The 120ft super yacht could be rented for $3,000 an hour and could host 80 people. Food and drinks cost extra, and you needed to also pay for a waitperson for every ten guests due to safety and service practices. The total cost of the party was $20,000, which admittedly is a lot of money. However, when you break it down to $250 a head it

While most people have been on a boat on the harbour, not many people have been on a super yacht

was a lot more palatable, especially as our clients typically pay us between $15,000 and $25,000 to search for, locate and negotiate on a property which may then save them $50,000 to $100,000. Also, our referral partners may send us up to ten clients a year - so it was a great way of saying thank you.

There were four things I learnt on that super yacht night:

☑   While most people have been on a boat on the harbour, not many people have been on a super yacht – it's next level luxury and an unbelievable experience. The service was exceptional, as was the food and drinks. Having a Christmas party on a super yacht was way better than holding it in any private dining room of a fancy restaurant everyone has been to

☑   You really do need 80 people to fill a super yacht of that size. With five different decks on multiple levels, a smaller group would have dampened the atmosphere.

☑   I might be good at networking and socialising, but trying to mingle with 80 people to say *"Hello, thank you, how's your portfolio going and how else can I assist you?"* was very hard and extremely tiring. It was difficult to give everyone the quality time I wanted to

☑   I loved it – how can I do it again, and again?

When I next spoke to my new best friend, I discovered that while it costs $3,000 to hire the boat for an hour, or $12,000 for four hours, the 24-hour cost is 'only' $25,000. Yes, it sounds like a lot, but once you've hired it for eight hours, the next 16 hours are free!

And then something else occurred to me. It also has five bedrooms (or cabins) and sleeps 10 people. So just like the boat syndicate idea, I asked myself "Why pay for the whole boat if I can't use the whole boat in one go?" Why not hire the boat with four other couples, or businesses, and split everything five ways?

We could have a party for 80 people on a Friday from 5 to 10pm. After last drinks, we could drop the guests off and then ten of us stay on board overnight. We would wake up on the harbour and then go for a morning swim followed by breakfast created by a personal chef. And that's not all. We would then do another party from 12 to 5pm for another 80 guests.

Each share, or couple, would get 16 invitations (80 people, divided by five equals 16) for both parties that comes to 32 invitations - and a free overnight stay. The cost of 24 hours on the super yacht (with upgraded food and catering for 160) would be around $50,000, or $10,000 per share.

So, for half the cost of me hosting my own party I could have 24 hours on the boat, I could invite 32 people instead of 80, but I would then have 128 (160 minus 32) new people I could meet. I ended up offering the other four shares to referral partners who we already worked with so a lot of the 128 other guests I either already knew, would have invited myself anyway, or was glad to meet as prospective new clients. The same worked for the other referral partners in meeting my clients, so it was a win-win all around and an amazing place to host a party.

This might be a business justification for making the sums work on a super yacht, but it can be justified for personal use. If you're not going to use a super yacht every day, then why pay for it every day?

I've either run my own event or been at someone else's event probably in excess of 25 times and have been fortunate to experience most of the super yachts on Sydney Harbour that are available for hire. As much as I love them - and would jump at the chance to own one to hang out on more often - I'm actually glad that I don't bring my cheque book out with me at night when I'm drinking, or in the sober light of day don't pursue the dream any further.

One birthday I happened to be at the Australia Super Yacht Rendezvous on the Gold Coast with a friend and we came across a very old secondhand 125-foot super yacht. It was up for sale for $1.8m, a similar price to the next brand new 52-foot syndicate boat that we, at the time, were about to upgrade to. Sure, it was secondhand but at 125 feet we could live on it! Four shares of $450,000 each and we would get it for a week every month.

However, it would need three full-time crew plus major maintenance considering its age, so the ongoing cost would probably have been $750,000 a year. Luckily, sense prevailed and we didn't buy it – what an expensive nightmare that could have been. As soon as we bought it, we would probably have had to put it on the market again because something like that can take several years to sell.

Many super yacht owners do put their boats up for charter (or rent) and could well turn a profit, allowing them to enjoy their boats 'for free' in the downtimes. However, you would need some very deep pockets to afford the capital cost in the first place, and then the ongoing expenses. The sun isn't always shining (even on a multimillion dollar super yacht) and having a few seasons of bad weather - or a global health pandemic - could leave an owner with a major liability afloat.

Since then, we've priced doing a week away in Europe to cruise St Tropez, Cannes and the other popular Mediterranean ports, which would probably work out around $200,000, $40,000 per couple, or $20,000 each. Yes, it's a lot of money, but much better to rent one for a week than be anchored down with one full time.

On the topic of international travel, I did meet another new 'best friend' in the boating world, this time one who runs super yachts in Croatia where boats are definitely more affordable. A brand new 150-foot boat with 18 cabins costs $7,000 per cabin a week. Admittedly it wasn't quite the top end luxury and service of the boats in Sydney Harbour, but given you can go to a different port each night and sample local restaurants, it would still be an amazing experience. At $3,500 a person for a seven-night luxury holiday, it is definitely a cheaper way to live like a multimillionaire.

RESOURCES - HIRING A SUPERYACHT

Jo Howard is my 'best friend' when it comes to super yachts and I've hired many from him over a number of years. He really knows his boats and the level of service that is required.

He runs a luxury yacht agency called Ocean Alliance, providing bespoke, unforgettable entertainment on the water. Whether you're thinking of something local or international, they will design your time onboard to deliver entertainment and enjoyment, in a relaxed setting which inspires amazing memories.

Luxury yachting is definitely one of the eight wonders of the world.

www.oceanalliance.com

RESOURCES – BUYING A SHARE IN A SYNDICATED BOAT

I met Andy Young back in 2013 when I was looking for an upgrade to the speed boat and needed something bigger that would suit both family and corporate environments.

He runs a business called BSA which offers boating enthusiasts an exciting and worry-free option in boat ownership, for a fraction of the normal cost and hassle. They have managed more than 100 syndicated boats in a variety of luxury boat brands, styles and sizes

You are not only buying a share in a syndicated boat but complete peace of mind and a boating lifestyle that is totally stress and hassle free. You arrive at your boat to begin a day, a weekend or a week on board and your boat is exceptionally clean, fuelled, checked and ready to go. When you return, you simply step off and they take care of the rest.

www.boatingsyndicationaustralia.com

CHAPTER 6
TAKING TO THE SKIES

HOW TO GET YOUR HANDS ON A PRIVATE HELICOPTER

Flying or being flown in a chopper has definitely got to be one of life's luxuries. Not having to worry about finding a runway means you can literally drop in anywhere. However, paying for the fuel isn't cheap, let alone the $1m to more than $10m purchase price of a private helicopter and the ongoing safety and maintenance requirements.

Having said that, flying in a chopper can still be attainable for as little as $5,000 for a whole year of flying.

Despite being scared of heights, I decided a chopper would be a good way to conquer my fears

Despite being scared of heights, in 2013 I decided a chopper would be a good way to conquer my fears and to find a new hobby. A mate of mine had previously got his light aircraft license, but I found that those little planes suddenly dropped and rose in the sky, which didn't help my vertigo. Choppers, on the other hand, seemed to be a lot more stable.

The main training ground for wannabe pilots is luckily not at Sydney International Airport where they could cause air traffic chaos, but in Bankstown, about 30 to 60 minutes west of Sydney's CBD depending on traffic.

Students learn in a pretty basic helicopter, often a Robinson R22, which starts up a bit like a lawnmower. It's a two-seater with dual controls – they're not going to let you loose in a chopper by yourself with no training! But even these cost a few hundred thousand dollars, so owning one would be a bit like having another Ferrari or Bentley in the garage.

Helicopter lessons are around $500 an hour, which seemed pretty expensive to me initially. However, I realised if I did that every month for 10 months of the year for $5,000, that would more than cover the cost of the chopper, an instructor and fuel. Given it can take an hour to get there, half an hour of messing around before and after, an hour to fly, plus an hour to get back, it's pretty much a half-day adventure. So even if I really did enjoy taking the controls of a helicopter, I probably would only have time to do it once a month anyway.

Renting a chopper for $5,000 a year wouldn't even compare to the cost of buying one. I might be only guessing, but I'm sure it would be 10 to 20 times more expensive than a service on a car with all the safety and maintenance requirements of the Civil Aviation Safety Authority. The cost of instructors, however, is almost negligible as there are so many wanting to build up their hours so they can get more lucrative commercial pilot licenses. So, whether you have your own license, or need someone next to you, it doesn't really matter.

Here are two of my favourite trips you can do in a chopper from Sydney:

- One hour at $500 – Get to Bankstown early in the morning when there isn't much wind about on a bright and sunny blue-sky day. Take off and fly over Sydney Olympic Park to Rhodes, turn right and follow the Parramatta River all the way to the CBD. Fly over the Harbour Bridge, wave to the bridge climbers, then travel through the harbour to Watsons Bay and out to North Head, checking out the commuters on the Manly Ferry below. Follow the coastline up the Northern Beaches, looking out for whales and dolphins along the way, up to Palm Beach. For the return, either choose the same route back, or for a bit of variety fly over the beautiful Ku-ring-gai Chase National Park, Cottage Point and Berowra Creek.

- Two hours at $1,000 – Fly up to the Central Coast and Caves Beach Resort, making sure to call them on the way and ask permission to land in their cliff top car park. Jump out of the chopper and pop into the pub for a chicken schnitzel, chips and a coke zero (or a beer if you want the instructor to chauffeur you back). Two hours can be a long time flying and can put a strain on the wrists and your concentration if you haven't flown much before, but it's a great catchup if you missed your regular flight the month before.

No doubt the uber wealthy would look down on Robinson R22 pilots, a bit like a Ferrari owner might brush off a scooter driver who's getting in the way of his speed run into the city. So, if you want an upgrade and are seeking some more prestige and comfort, then you can rent a mega chopper. That comes with the convenience of flying from Sydney International Airport, and not having to traipse all the way to Bankstown and back.

A client of mine lives on an acreage 15 to 20kms from Sydney's CBD and doesn't even go to the airport to meet the chopper, it comes to him. The pilot lands in his back garden and takes his family of four off to lunch in the Hunter Valley, and then back home again, for just under $3,000 – now that's affordable luxury! Rates for the more luxurious choppers are around $700, or more, an hour and can fit four to five passengers.

In my opinion, unless you use one weekly for work or pleasure and you have it permanently parked in your back garden, it just doesn't make any sense to own a helicopter. I'm pretty sure there are enough rentals around for you to find one whenever you wanted to take off.

However, if you're Dick Smith, you probably do have a valid reason for owning your own chopper (he did the first solo trans-Atlantic flight by helicopter in 1982, the first solo circumnavigation by helicopter in 1983, flew the first helicopter to the North Pole in 1987, then completed the first circumnavigation landing at both poles in 1989, and achieved the first east-west circumnavigation by helicopter in 1995).

THE PATHWAY TO BECOMING A PRIVATE JET SETTER

Back in the UK, when I was in my early twenties, I happened to know a very wealthy family. One day, I very unsubtly asked the mother *"Of all the material luxuries you get to enjoy, which one gives you the most pleasure?"*

Her answer was - their private jet. There was a private airport five minutes from their house on the outskirts of London and in the time it would take most people to navigate the M25 (known to locals to be more of a car park than a motorway) and then check in and go through security at an airport, they could be lounging on their super yacht in the south of France, or lazing in their Swiss ski chalet.

I wasn't crude enough to ask the cost of buying (and running) a private jet that was large enough to fit their family and close friends, but I'm sure it wasn't cheap. That kind of luxury is well beyond the lifelong savings of even moderately wealthy people.

I believe that even most ultra high net worth individuals who globetrot in private jets would still rent or lease out their jets (as they likely do with their boats) to minimise the cost of ownership - or to maybe just break even. To keep a private jet ready to go on the runway (just for yourself) is a folly purely for the mega wealthy.

Just like the luxury assets I've mentioned previously, there is a way to sample the jet setting scene, without actually buying a private jet.

Consider a private jet syndicate – here's one of the programs:

- Four owners in the syndicate

- 150 hours of flight time per year

- Five-year membership

- USD $2.5m per share (USD $10m for the whole plane)

- AUD $165,000 per quarter for five years including ongoings

- No hidden additional fees

Personally, I would struggle to justify $55,000 a month (or $3.3m over five years) for ongoings, let alone paying for the more than $3m capital cost, but that's mainly because I would only be using a private jet for leisure. However, if you had a high revenue national or international business and needed your management team all over the place, then it would make a lot more sense joining a syndicate than owning a plane outright.

For those who fly for fun, then I think the rental model is probably the way to go. A very luxurious 10-seater jet, such as a Challenger 604, would cost around $20,000 to $25,000 for a Sydney to Melbourne return flight, or Sydney to the Gold Coast. At $2,000 to $2,500 per person that could be fairly affordable, especially if you were celebrating a major event or motivating a high performing sales team. Recently, some friends of mine flew from Sydney to Mudgee for lunch for $7,500, which equated to $750 each for 10 people.

Despite the luxury, I'm not the type of passenger who would like to fly back after a boozy business lunch. For not a lot extra (if the jet didn't have a follow-on booking) you could pay for the pilot and crew to stay overnight at the destination and then fly you back in the morning, which would extend your adventure. Otherwise, you would be paying $20,000 to $25,000 for a one-way flight and the jet would make the return flight empty.

For those on a budget, there are companies around that will try and on-sell that empty return flight at a discount. This can be great alternative if your timetable and (friends) are flexible enough to accommodate a flight at short notice. However, it could be tricky to find two empty flights to connect to make a return journey.

Another possibility is to buy a single seat on a private jet that someone else may have hired. Some high flying passengers aren't too fussed on flying with an extra passenger because they would rather sell some of the spare seats to reduce their cost. This could be a great way to see if flying in a private jet is for you. This way of flying is much more prevalent in the USA and is the way a lot of businesspeople travel stateside. Australia, however, doesn't yet have the same level of population or demand.

HOW TO FLY BUSINESS (OR FIRST) CLASS AT ECONOMY PRICES

Who wouldn't want to fly up the front of the plane in business or first class with free French champagne and lobster? It is possible, and all it takes is a change in the way you spend. That is, spend the same money you already do, but just in a different way.

Like most people around the world, I use credit cards to pay for my general personal and business spending. It's easier, and more secure, than paying cash and I get the benefit of frequent flyer points.

Spend the same money you already do, but just in a different way

I used to get around 100,000 to more than 200,000 points a year as virtually everything I bought was paid for with credit cards. As long as I paid it off every month, it wouldn't really cost me any extra, apart from the annual fee.

Airline frequent flyer points were always a mystery to me and something I couldn't be bothered spending. So, each year I would convert 100,000 credit card points to $1,000 of David Jones or Myers vouchers. I'd give them to my wife and I didn't really see where the money went.

Eventually, as my business became more successful and my property portfolio grew, I ended up having more time (and money) to travel overseas. I struggled to justify paying $5,000 for a business class flight to Hong Kong, Singapore, or Bangkok when I could fly economy for $1,000. Granted, it was never a fun flight, especially overnight or if you sat next to a nightmare passenger, but I figured it was worth it if I had an extra $4,000 of spending money at the other end.

My mindset changed when I would see my business colleagues, who were flying at the 'pointy end' of the plane, stepping off looking completely refreshed - and sometimes even showered! Despite their enviably refreshed state, I still asked them how they justified spending all that extra money. "Oh, I don't pay for it in cash, it's all frequent flyer points," one of them told me "We put all the business turnover through the credit cards and then my assistant is a whizz at finding the connections online".

I didn't have an assistant, and I certainly didn't know a whizz at finding flights online until I came across Steve Hui from iflyflat.com.au aka The Points Whisperer. Pay him a small fee, or a percentage of the money he saves you, and he'll find the flights and make all the bookings. And as a bonus, he'll even teach you which credit cards give you the most points per dollar spent, which are the easiest airline programs to get flights on, and how to get more out of your existing credit card spending. As a result, for many years I've flown between 10 and 15 times a year overseas, always in business or first class.

Once I had the whole of first class to myself flying back from Greece on Thai Airways (it was an older style plane, so not super luxurious and it did get a bit lonely – but that's a first world problem).

Flying from Sydney to Hong Kong is often 90,000 points going direct in business class, or 176,000 points via Singapore in first class. The first class suites are unbelievable (and often much better than my hotel room anyway) so I'm more than happy to spend another few hours in the air. Another perk is that they collect you by private buggy, take you to the first class lounge and once there serve you lobster and Krug champagne.

For those people who fly to Europe, you could pay 290,000 points between Sydney and London in Business and less than 330,000 points to fly in First Class, making First Class a relative bargain.

Different airlines charge different points to fly to the same destination and they change over time, hence why I need to use Steve who is on top of this for me, rather than trying to learn a set formula and then keep repeating.

RESOURCES – HOW TO FLY IN THE POINTY END OF A PLANE

I was Steve Hui's fifth customer and I absolutely love his business and I'm sure you will too. Want to put flying in the pointy-end at economy prices into action?

iFLYflat – The Points Whisperer - an exclusive travel company specialising in:

☑   Using your own credit card and frequent flyer points to fly in First and Business class, and

☑   Provide tailored advice to earn maximum points from all sources.

Most people who have points struggle to find and book the best seats, and are unaware they can often earn significantly more points from their every-day credit card spending.

www.iflyflat.com.au

Mention you discovered this via *How to live the life of a multimillionaire* book for enhanced care.

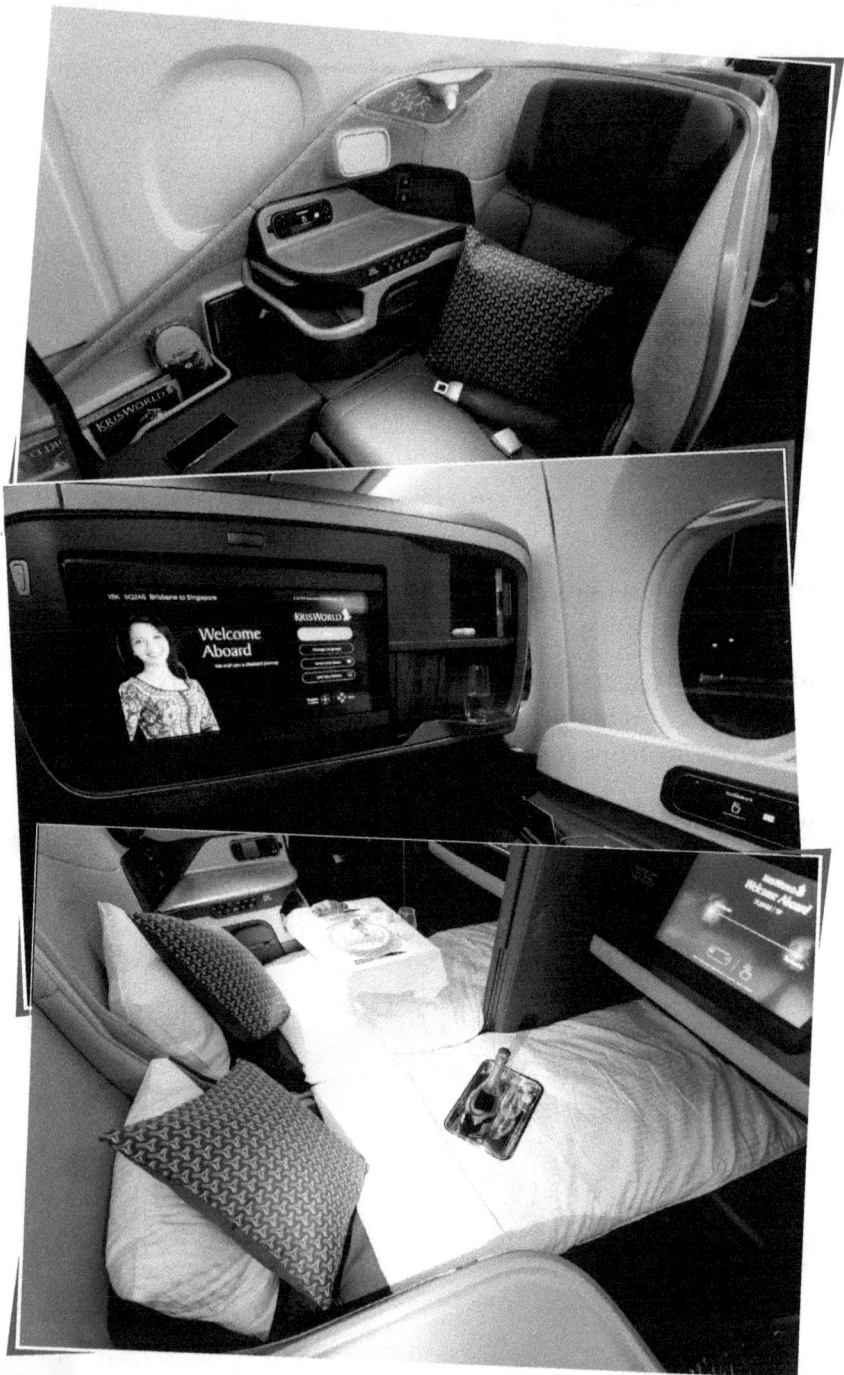

RESOURCES - FLY IN A PRIVATE JET

If you want to fly in a private jet without buying it, or even paying full price to rent it, then Luke Hampshire from Airly could well be the person you need to speak to.

He's got an app that will allow you to search for the empty return leg flights - when someone has paid full price but only needs to go one way. That's a seriously cheap private jet experience.

As more and more people get to see the benefits of flying private, it should get easier and easier to fly, especially between our main capital cities.

www.airly.com

CHAPTER 7
WHERE TO FROM HERE?

As I said at the start of this book, money is not going to make you happier, but you can definitely have some fun with it. While I'm a strong believer in people following their careers, working hard throughout their lives, and not being too material - I also believe in living for today.

The old strategy of working until you are 65 to then go on an around-the-world trip just doesn't work these days. So many people don't get to retire until they're in their seventies as they can't afford to do it any earlier. And it's worth considering what that retiree adventure would look like. I'm not sure how many 65-year-olds will be bungy jumping off Victoria Falls in Africa or leaping out of a plane over Hawaii.

It might sound like a cliche, but I believe you need to live in the moment and that means striking a balance between enjoying today, and saving for tomorrow for you (and your family).

Hopefully this book has demonstrated that you don't actually need as much money as you might have thought to experience the finer things in life. And if you're fortunate enough to have money left over after implementing these strategies, then you might be able to give back to your local community or to assist those less fortunate in other countries.

To do the things mentioned in this book, you will of course still need to have additional funds - and that's where I come in. I am here assist you too – to help you buy your next home, a holiday home, or to start building a passive property portfolio that will work for you.

Ultimately, it's not about what you earn, it's what you do with the money you do make that counts. If you take some action today, you will be putting your financial foot in the right direction for tomorrow.

It's not about what you earn, it's what you do with the money you do make that counts

FOR MORE INFORMATION

Chris Gray and the team at Your Empire can help you:

- Purchase your dream family home
- Buy the perfect investment property at the right price
- Renovate your property for a fixed price, without all the headaches
- Get your investment property managed by leading property managers
- Learn how to become an expert property investor yourself, through some of Australia's most comprehensive online learning tools

phone:	+61 2 9994 8944
email:	info@yourempire.com.au
office:	Level 11 66 Clarence St Sydney NSW 2000
mail:	PO Box N64 Grosvenor Place PO NSW 1220
websites:	www.yourempire.com.au www.chrisgray.com.au

WORKING WITH CHRIS GRAY

Chris Gray is available as an expert on property, wealth creation and living life like a millionaire for television, radio, print, online and podcasts.

You can contact Chris directly:

chris.gray@yourempire.com.au

ABOUT THE AUTHOR

Chris Gray is one of Australia's leading independent investment property experts, giving home buyers and investors simple yet powerful strategies to create wealth and lifestyle options through property.

Chris is a 10-year veteran television host with Sky News Business and has appeared as a property expert with all the major television networks, radio and publications within Australia (along with international guest appearances as well).

Having started his career as a qualified accountant, Chris retired from full time work at age 31 when he realised his property portfolio was making him more than his job. Chris has since grown his property portfolio to a value of circa $20 million.

Now living in Sydney with his family, Chris continues to share his expertise through his Buyer's Agency, Your Empire, as well as being a sought after speaker, presenter and educator.

Discover more:

www.chrisgray.com.au
www.yourempire.com.au

www.ingramcontent.com/pod-product-compliance
Lightning Source LLC
Chambersburg PA
CBHW070939210326
41520CB00021B/6973